A Letter to My Sister

THE COLUMBA SERIES

1. ON CONTEMPLATING GOD. William of St. Thierry
2. ON JESUS AT TWELVE YEARS OLD. St. Aelred of Rievaulx
3. THE SCHOOL OF SELF-KNOWLEDGE.
4. ON THE NATURE AND DIGNITY OF LOVE. William of St. Thierry
5. LETTER TO MY SISTER. Saint Aelred of Rievaulx.
6. THE STEPS OF HUMILTY. St. Bernard.
7. LETTERS OF SPIRITUAL DIRECTION. Bossuet.

Saint Aelred of Rievaulx

A Letter to My Sister

*Translated from the Latin and Middle English
Versions and edited by*
GEOFFREY WEBB AND ADRIAN WALKER

London
The Saint Austin Press
MMI

Nihil Obstat: JOHANNES M. T. BARTON, S.T.D., L.S.S.
Imprimatur: E. MORROGH BERNARD, *Vic. Gen.*
Westmonasterii, die 26a Mai, 1955

The Saint Austin Press
296 Brockley Road
London
SE4 2RA
Tel +44 (0)20 8692 6009
Fax +44 (0)20 8469 3609
Email: books@saintaustin.org
Website: www.saintaustin.org

ISBN 1901157 52 0

First published by Mowbrays in 1957
Design and typography of this edition © The Saint Austin Press, 2001.

All rights reserved.
A CIP record of this book is available.

"The publishers have made considerable efforts to trace the current copyright holders of this work, first published nearly 50 years ago, but have been unable to do so. If they have unwittingly infringed copyright, they will be happy to honour any reasonable claims from copyright holders who contact them in writing at the above address."

Printed by Newton Design & Print Ltd, London, UK.   www.newtondp.co.uk

INTRODUCTION

SAINT AELRED'S letter to his sister was written about the year 1160, when he was already suffering from the many infirmities which were to allow him only seven more years of life on this earth. His biographer, Walter Daniel, tells us that he had ordered a cell to be made close by the infirmary at Rievaulx, in a corner of which he established an inner closet. Here he would pray and write, and it was here that he composed his thirty-three homilies on Isaiah, the dialogue *On Spiritual Friendship*, and 'a book to his sister, the chaste virgin who was a recluse, in which he traced the course of this kind of profession from the ardour of the entrance into the same, to its perfection'.

This is all that we know for certain about Aelred's sister. Her name, the location of her hermitage, all details concerning her have disappeared. Nonetheless, the letter provides some illuminating, even touching references to their childhood spent together in Northumberland, before Aelred left for the court of King David of Scotland. One may suppose that Aelred was somewhat older than his sister, for 'she wept over him sometimes and reproached him when she was but a young girl', for adolescent misdemeanours. When he wrote this letter, Aelred was fifty, and his sister had been a recluse already for some years.

To judge by Saint Aelred's opening words, she had been asking him to write her a rule of life for some years past. When at last he did so it was to an ageing woman that he addressed it, and less for her benefit than for that of those younger than herself who might be attracted by the recluse's life. Aelred collated his 'rule' from the fathers and from the Rule of Saint Benedict which he himself followed, as interpreted by the order of Citeaux. Thus we find that the liturgical legislation of Saint Benedict is embodied in this rule for anchoresses, and Cistercian influence is noticeable in the injunctions to avoid receiving guests or pupils, although this is only the logical consequence of the anchoress having only sufficient for her own needs. Guests could be better cared for in the monastery guesthouses, and we may be fairly sure that her cell would not be far from a monastery by the fact that Aelred insists that 'an elderly monk from a large monastery' is to be her confessor and spiritual director.

It is a matter for conjecture what rule Aelred's sister had been following hitherto. Aelred's rule is the first one written in England, being quoted in the later *Ancren Riwle*. But the eremitical life had been practised in this country since it was first evangelized. Possibly her brother had little to add to the recluse's rule of life other than the stress which he lays on the need for a complete severance from the world. The chief evil in the eremitical life as practised in his time comes out clearly enough in Aelred's description of those recluses who are perpetually at their window either gossiping, or scolding over a business deal, or berating their pupils, or holding converse with undesirables of all sorts. And so Aelred insists that his sister should choose 'an honest old woman . . . one not given to wrangling and tale bearing and gadding about, but manifestly of good life, whose duty it shall be to look after you and your dwelling, to see to the door and receive all who come, and to send away anyone whose company you had best avoid'. This servant is to have under her care a housemaid for the heavy work such as fetching wood and water, cooking and getting meals ready.

The first twenty chapters of Aelred's rule for his sister deal with the recluse's timetable, and general regulations for her life. The recluse's day, like that of the monks, begins a few hours after midnight. She rises to say Matins, and during the interval between Matins and Lauds (which were said at dawn) she spends her time in alternate periods of prayer, reading and work. She may recite the little office of Our Lady and the commemorations of the saints, but this is not of obligation. Such a *salubris alternatio* is designed, Aelred says, to recreate the spirit and to prevent accidie, that spiritual nausea which the fathers of the desert counted as their greatest temptation. The hermit, being 'abbot, prior and prefect in the cloister of his heart', needs an organized programme, but at the same time must consider the demands of both body and mind, and must not overtax either, as might well be the case in a day spent entirely without human companionship. The recluse, then, must become adept at alternating her pursuits so as to keep her spirit fresh and unwearied for long days spent wholly in the company of God. Lauds would be followed by Prime, which in turn was followed by some hours of reading and prayer until Terce (9 a.m.). The recluse betook herself to some form of manual work from Terce until Sext (12 noon) in the summer, and in winter until None (3 p.m.). Then came dinner which, in the summer months, was followed by a siesta. Work and prayer were resumed in the afternoon until Vespers. After that the recluse read from the lives of the fathers, those celebrated *Collationes* of Cassian which have given the name 'collation' to the monastic evening meal which occurred at the time of reading. In summer the recluse was to take care that she was in bed before sunset.

Aelred had stricter views on silence than the author of the *Ancren Riwle*. As far as possible he would have complete silence in the anchorage throughout Lent. From Easter to the feast of the Exaltation of the Holy Cross, on September 14th, the recluse is allowed to talk to her servant in the morning after Prime, and in the evening, between Vespers and collation. She is allowed to speak with visitors in the afternoon between None and Vespers. From the Exaltation of the Holy Cross until Lent the time for speaking with visitors is changed to the hours in the morning and early afternoon between Terce and None. She is always to receive them with her face veiled. As regards food and drink, Saint Benedict's rule is followed, and the anchoress may have a pound of bread a day, and a pint of drink. This ration may be consumed either at one meal or divided between the two meals normally allowed. In Lent there is only one meal a day, after Vespers, and on the vigils of saints' days, on Wednesdays and on Emberdays, the recluse fasts as in Lent. On Fridays she fasts on bread and water. But on all other days she has two meals, namely, dinner consisting of vegetables cooked in oil, butter or milk, with fresh fruits in season, and supper or 'collation' composed of a little fish or cheese. The hour of dinner varies. From Easter to Pentecost it is at Sext, and from the Exaltation of the Holy Cross to Lent at None. On fast days, a rest is permitted after dinner and between Matins and Prime.

Aelred commends the Lenten fast to his sister by recalling the time-honoured examples of Moses who fasted for forty days before receiving the law, of Elijah who did likewise on his journey to Horeb, and of Our Lord Himself in the desert. It is the fast which holy church imposes on all her children, for it is the greatest remedy against temptation. For the religious, it is the necessary guard of chastity. It is, he explains, a great mystery, for our first dwelling was in paradise, before we came to this world full of sorrows. Our third and last home will be in heaven, with the angels and blessed spirits. The mystical significance of forty days is, then, that they symbolize the middle time between the original paradise and the ultimate heaven—from fall to last judgment. Human fragility needs to be reminded that it is expelled from paradise, and not yet come to heaven; and Lent reminds us that we are fasting for the joys of heaven. As the priest says on Ash Wednesday when he puts ashes on the heads of the faithful, 'Dust thou art, and unto dust thou shalt return', thus showing us how we are fallen and expelled from paradise. The veil which is drawn across the sanctuary of the church during the Easter triduum shows us how the vision of God is denied us in this exile. For all, Lent is a time for special custody of the eye and heart, but for the recluse it is the time most specially welcomed as an opportunity for pleasing Christ, her husband, by the fervour of her prayers. Lent for her is like the time of betrothal, in which she longs for the embrace of Christ at the marriage feast.

The middle-English translation of the letter from chapter twenty-one onwards (which the present rendering follows) deals with the virtues and prayer. It opens on the subject of chastity, and with the conversational simplicity which one would expect in a letter written to a near relative, Aelred goes on to speak of that chaste austerity which a recluse is to observe in her dress, her surroundings, her food and so on. A particularly delightful allegory of fine linen leads on to the subject of clothes. A recluse must make herself a wedding gown of virtues, beautiful in its many-coloured diversity as that worn by the queen-mother in Ahab's wedding psalm. The gown must have a golden hem, for the hem, being 'the last end of the cloth', is an image of Saint Paul's *finis precepti est charitas*—'the purpose of our charge is charity'.

Charity is love, and love is twofold—namely, the love of God, and the love of our fellow christians. Even the recluse is bound to love her fellow men, and the precise definition of how far such a one may go in such matters as alms-giving is something which seems to have exercised the mind of

Aelred's sister. 'You ask me what kind of alms deeds you may do, who have forsaken the world.' The answer is one of rare beauty. . . . 'Bind all this world together in your heart, with a bond of pity and love.' A recluse has Mary's part—to pray: Martha's part is not denied to be good, but the special wedding gift of Christ's spouses is 'to hear devoutly His word and His commands'.

Aelred then develops a meditation on Our Lord's life in the gospel, which is surely one of the most moving ever written. The expression which is rendered in middle-English as 'the mind of Christ's benefits' is that *memoria* already rich with connotations from the Mass. . . . 'Mindful, therefore, O Lord, not only of Christ's blessed passion, but also of His resurrection from the dead and His glorious ascension into heaven. . . .' To remember the life of Christ is to be brought into His real and living presence as in liturgical prayer. The presence of God is found in that memorial of Christ's life, 'the true gospel'. As one reads the first part of the threefold meditation, one can see Aelred fitting his sister into the gospel context. One can indeed visualize her accompanying Our Lady to Bethlehem, and over the hills of Judea. At the last supper she has Judas to contend with in person, as he 'grouses at her, saying "Why this waste?" ' at her anointing Our Lord's head with all the love she can find in the alabaster box of her heart.

One can see how profoundly Aelred himself lived the gospel, but even more perhaps, one is struck by the depth of his self-revelation. The second part of the meditation, which is complemented by his confession at the beginning of the dialogue *On Spiritual Friendship*, is part of his autobiography. The story of the monk who was tempted is part of his story. His frequent declarations of God's mercy, even when damning the sinner, and of the sheer gratuitousness of His justification of good men, are witnesses to Aelred's own anguish at the thought of judgment. The harsh Augustinian conception of predestination is something which he would often have wished to palliate, but his own devotion to Augustine as an authority could never allow him to do so. And although God's universal salvific will is thereby put out of its true place for him, still the unsolved problem could urge him to such acts of pure love and hope and trust in God's mercy as his prayer at the cross in chapter twelve. Here we see the depth of his humble and loving abandonment to God's will.

The medieval translation of the letter into English occurs in the Vernon MS. as an introduction to various other treatises on the enclosed life. Horstmann, who edited the Rule in 1884 (*Englische Studien*, Band VII, Heilbronn) is of the opinion that the Vernon MS. was designed for a convent of nuns. In the sixteenth century the Latin text of the letter was mistakenly attributed to Saint Augustine. For this reason it is to be found in Migne P.L. 32, cols. 1451 to 1465. The present edition follows Thomas N., the English translator, with as little modification as possible, but with enough, it is hoped, to make the work assimilable to the reader unacquainted with the English of that period. We should like, finally, to express our grateful thanks to Père Charles Dumont who first introduced us to the work.

G. W.
A. W.

Easter, 1955

CONTENTS

CHAP.		PAGE
	Introduction	5
I.	A precious treasure in a frail vessel	15
II.	The chastity of the saints	17
III.	On true discretion	20
IV.	On meekness	22
V.	The wedding garment	24
VI.	Love of God and love of men	26
VII.	Martha and Mary: action and contemplation	28
VIII.	Meditation on things past: From the Annunciation to the Nativity	32
IX.	From the flight into Egypt to Our Lord's ministry	34
X.	Holy Thursday	39
XI.	The Passion	42
XII.	A prayer at the Passion	46
XIII.	The Resurrection	47
XIV.	Meditation on things present: God's patience with sinful men	49
XV.	God's mercy, grace and goodness	52
XVI.	Meditation on things to come: The thought of judgment	55
XVII.	Doomsday	57
XVIII.	The kingdom of eternal bliss	60
	Notes	63

A LETTER TO HIS SISTER

I

A PRECIOUS TREASURE IN A FRAIL VESSEL

LET her now hear and understand me well, whoever she may be that forsakes this world and chooses the solitary life, desiring to be hidden and unseen; wishing as a body dead to this world to be buried in a cave with Christ. Let her, I say, ask herself frequently why she prefers the solitary life to living in the fellowship of men. For the Apostle says: 'A wise maiden studies and thinks upon the things of God'[1] —that is to say, how she may please God so as to be holy in body and soul.

This virtue, that is to say of chastity, is a willing sacrifice and a free offering to God, to which no law drives us, no need constrains us, and no command binds us. And therefore Christ says in the Gospel: 'Whoever may take this virtue, let him take it.'[2] Lord, who may take it? Surely, he only in whom God has inspired such a will, and given the grace and power to act accordingly. Therefore, do you, maiden, before all things, and with all the devotion of your heart, commend your good purpose to Him Who has inspired it in you. And with constant prayer beseech Him that that which is impossible for you by nature, may be made easy for you by His grace.

Think how precious a treasure in how frail a vessel you have to bear about, and what a crown, what a reward of bliss is afforded to us by chastity faithfully preserved. And consider also what pain, what confusion, what eternal damnation it brings upon us if it be lost. And what more precious treasure can you imagine, for this buys heaven for us, while it fills the angels with delight; for Christ desires it with all His heart, and God is drawn to love a chaste soul and to give ... what gift? I make bold to say—Himself, and all that is His or ever was. And thus the sweetness of your maidenhood wafting up to heaven as a sweet savour, ensures that our true king and lord, Almighty God, has a desire for your fairness.

Behold now what a spouse you have chosen, what a friend you have won! Surely He is fairer than any man that ever was born, fairer than the sun, and surpassing the fairness of the stars. His breath is sweeter than honey, and His heritage above honey and all sweetness. Length of everlasting days is in His right hand,[3] and in His left hand are all riches and bliss. He has chosen you to be his wife; but He will not crown you before your strength is proved. The Book says: 'He that is not tempted, is not proved.'[4] Now, maidenhood is gold, and your cell is a furnace; the blower to melt this gold is the devil, and the fire is temptation. A maiden's flesh is, as it were, an earthen vessel in which the gold is to be purified: and therefore, if this vessel were to burst under the great heat of the fire of temptation, the gold would pour out, and even the most skilful craftsman could never make the vessel as it was originally.

Thinking on these things, a holy woman must see that she keeps with all diligence and holy fear that precious treasure of maidenhood, which is of so much value and profit when it is possessed, but which can never be recovered when it is lost. Let her consider continually for whose wedding chamber it is that she is made bright and beautiful, for whose embrace she is made ready. Let her keep before her eyes the Lamb that she must follow wherever He may go—that is, Christ. Let her gaze on the blessed Mary with the tympany of chastity, leading as it were the dance of holy virgins, and singing that sweet song that none may sing but pure virgins, both men and women; for it is written of them: 'These are they that have not defiled themselves . . . these are pure virgins.'[5]

Wherefore it is of great importance that a holy maid should remember that all her members are hallowed to God, incorporated in Christ, and dedicated to the Holy Ghost. And, surely, it is very wrong to give over to the devil that which belongs to Christ. And therefore she should be ashamed indeed to let her body be defiled in any way whatsoever. Let her, then, strive with all her heart to preserve her cleanness and chastity, and to keep this aim always in her heart, so that she, hungering, as it were, for the perfection of this virtue, thinks hunger a great delight, and considers poverty as the greatest of riches. In meat and drink, in sleeping and in speaking, always let her dread the staining of her chastity, lest, if she give more than is due to her flesh, she give strength to her adversary, and nourish the enemy that lives within her.

II

THE CHASTITY OF THE SAINTS

WHEN you lie down on your bed at night, sister, commend your chastity to your God, and then, armed with the sign of the cross, consider how you have lived that day. And if in word or deed or thought you have offended your God, cry to Him for mercy, and sigh and smite your breast. If you have been idle or neglectful, or if you have passed the bounds of due need in meat or drink, then you must pray for the mercy of your God. And so, with this evening sacrifice, let sleep find you reconciled with your spouse.

Remember sometimes the blessed virgins of long ago. Think how the blessed Saint Agnes despised gold and silver, precious gowns and priceless stones, and all the pomp of worldly glory and happiness as if it were but dung. When she was called to trial, she did not shirk it. The tyrant flattered her, but she defied him. He threatened her and she laughed him to scorn, dreading more that he would spare her than that he would slay her. She was a blessed maiden indeed, she who turned a whore-house into an oratory. An angel entered the prison with her, and turned darkness into light, and slew with sudden death him who pursued her chastity. And therefore if you will only pray and cry to God with bitter tears against the tempter of lechery, without doubt the angel who accompanied Agnes will not be far from you. And it was surely fitting that no material fire should burn that holy maid in whom charity had kindled its fire and the flames of uncleanness were quenched. And as often as any burning temptation comes upon you, as often as any wicked spirit urges you to unlawful lusts, remember that He is also present Who tries the reins of your heart, and that whatever you do or think is known to Him. Have also reverence for the good angel whom you know has been set to look after you, and answer your tempter in this way: 'My lover is an angel of God, and with great jealousy he keeps my body.'[6] And if these temptations continue, let stricter abstinence help you, for when the flesh suffers under the rod of abstinence, there is no room, or very little, for the delights of the flesh.

Let no man flatter himself or fool himself in this matter, for without great contrition of heart and bodily penance, chastity may neither be won nor kept. I knew at one time a monk, who in the beginning of his conversion, perhaps through some stirring of the natural appetite, perhaps through some vicious habit previously formed, perhaps also through the suggestions of the wicked tempter—he, dreading that his purity might be assailed and lost, rose up against himself, and conceiving a terrible hatred of his own flesh, he desired nothing more than to put his body to torment and discomfort. And therefore he made his body lean by austerity, and in order to curb the unlawful motions of his flesh, he abstained even from the things that were needful for the body. But afterwards, when great feebleness compelled him to take more heed of his body, the flesh began to grow proud again, and to threaten to make an end of the peace that he had enjoyed for a while in chastity. And then what did he do but cast himself into freezing cold water, and shivering he cried out and prayed against his temptations. Another time he rubbed his body with nettles which stung him fiercely, but when all this proved insufficient, and the spirit of uncleanness assailed him in spite of all his efforts, he fell down before the feet of Jesus Christ as a last refuge, praying, weeping, sighing and beseeching that He would either heal him or kill him. Piteously and often he cried out to his Lord, as it says in the Book: 'I will never go hence, I will never have rest, I will never leave Thee, until Thou hast given me Thy blessing.'[7] And then the temptation ceased for a time, but security was still denied him. Ah, sweet God, what sorrow this wretch suffered, how he was tormented until he was at last granted such great joy in chastity that all the lusts that may be thought or spoken of could not have disturbed him. But even now that he is old and sick, that monk never flatters himself that he is safe from temptation.

And therefore, my dear sister, you must never be too sure of yourself, but you must always dread and suspect your own frailty. As a timorous dove, haunt the rivers of clear water, where you may see the reflection of the ravenous hawk when he flies above you, and beware! These rivers are the holy scriptures, that gush out from the well of wisdom that is Christ. These will show you not only the shadow of the devil's suggestion, but also advice and counsel for avoiding it. For there is nothing that so banishes wicked and unclean thoughts as does the reading of holy scripture; and a good woman—and especially a holy maiden—should give all her heart and mind to studying them, so that she may think of nothing but God's law. Let sleep find her thinking on holy scripture. And when she awakes from her sleep, let some phrase of holy teaching come into her mind. And while she is asleep, let some sentence stick in her memory from holy writings which will surely keep both her body and soul safe from harm while she sleeps.

III

ON TRUE DISCRETION

But it is a great shame that there are many who will not occupy themselves with spiritual things because of all kinds of false fears. They are afraid that they will fall into some great sickness as a result of abstinence, or of keeping long vigils in the service of God. And they are afraid that they will then be a burden to other men, and will themselves be in sorrow and trouble. But surely this is just our sinful excuse. For, Lord, how few there are nowadays that have a great fervour for holiness. We hold that we are all wise, that we are discreet in all things, that we are prudent and knowledgeable in all matters. So much do we dread discomfort and sickness of our body that we fear it before it comes. Yet any sickness of soul that we feel to be present, we take no heed of, as though it were better to suffer the burning fires of lechery than a little pain in our stomach. As though it were not better to avoid the unclean rebellions of the flesh by sickness of the body, than to be whole in body and to be overcome and made a slave by the lusts of our flesh. Lord, what does it matter whether it be abstinence or sickness that humbles our proud flesh, so long as chastity is preserved? But perhaps you will say that a man must be careful not to take too little notice of his body. If he has been brought up in comfort, might not the sickness he incurs through too much abstinence make it easier for foul lusts to make him their victim? And I answer that, if his flesh is suffering, sick and feeble, if his stomach is dry and his appetite has gone, be assured that any pleasures you might show him would not tempt him, but would rather be tedious and boring.

I once saw a man who did not know how to be chaste and continent, for in his youth he had been bound and overcome by evil habits. Nevertheless he at last took heed of his perilous state and began to be ashamed at his conduct. When he thought of his foul and sinful life, his heart began to burn within him as if it were on fire. And afterwards, being angry with himself, he began to fight against his own flesh so bitterly that he even avoided things that seem necessary for the body to have. Previously he had been merry and gay, but now he grew serious. Although he had always been chattering before, he now began to live in silence; and from that time no one saw him laughing and jesting, and no idle or unnecessary word was heard from his lips. He despised and scorned all worldly comforts and pleasures such as are found in sleeping, eating and drinking, and which might give his flesh some delight. To refrain the thoughts of his heart he was so careful and scrupulous that many people thought that he was lacking in moderation in his self-denial.

His mind was sad and his eyes downcast as he performed all his actions, whether it were sitting, walking or standing.

As he trembled and quaked, it seemed that he was already standing before the dreadful Judge on the last day. But there is no doubt that with these arms he won a glorious victory over the enemies which attacked his soul, and over the tyrant that had held him in bonds, the flesh. For in a short time he fell ill with a serious sickness of his stomach, and after a long illness the hour for his last sleep came. And with great feeling he said these words: 'Suffer a while, suffer ... Lo, where Jesus comes!' But I do not tell you of this to decry the goodness of moderation and discretion, the mother and nurse of all the virtues. I only say that we should do away with things that lead to serious sin—that is to say, gluttony, too much rest, and too much contact with those who are self-indulgent. For often we whiten our foul lusts and desires by falsely branding our actions with the name of moderation and discretion. But it is the right form of discretion to put the soul before the body, for since they are both in peril, and since the soul may not be saved unless the body undergoes some suffering, it is only reasonable that the body should be given second place so that the soul may be saved. I say these things to you, sister, so that you may never forget how much you must strive to remain chaste and clean; for this virtue of maidenly chastity, although it is the ornament and flower of all the virtues, dries up and fades away without meekness.

IV

ON MEEKNESS

THIS virtue of meekness is the firm foundation of every kind of virtue. Without it any progress you may make will disappear. The beginning of all sin is pride, which cast an angel out of heaven, and a man out of paradise. And although many deadly and poisonous branches spring from this accursed root, they are all divided into two kinds: into spiritual and bodily. Bodily pride is to be proud of bodily things; spiritual pride is to be proud of spiritual gifts. And furthermore, bodily pride is divided into two—boasting and vanity. It is vanity if a handmaiden of Christ has vainglory in her heart that she is noble and of good blood, and if because of this she takes delight in thinking that she has forsaken riches and nobility and given herself to a life of poverty. It is vanity if she thinks that she is wonderfully holy, and that she is to be praised for having forsaken marriage to the sons of wealthy men, and that she might have married so-and-so ... all this is vanity.

It is also a kind of vanity if you desire bodily fairness too much, or if you take too much pleasure in making your cell bright and comfortable with various paintings and hangings and other decorations. All these fancy things you must avoid as incompatible with your profession. How could you dare to glory in riches or in noble blood, when you long to be the spouse of Him Who became poor for us, although His are all the riches of the world—that is to say Christ? A poor mother, a poor maiden, a poor house He chose, and the narrowness of an ox's stall. And Lord, is it a great wonder, is it a reason for vainglory, that you have chosen not to wed a man's son because of the love and desire you feel to be Christ's spouse? Is it a great wonder that you have renounced the pleasures of the flesh for the sweet delights of maidenhood? Could anyone think it marvellous that you have exchanged things that perish and corrupt for the everlasting bliss and riches of heaven? Should you have vainglory although you have done all this? Holy Scripture says: 'He that glories, let him glory in the Lord.'[8] Sister, if you are happy about these things, make sure that your joy and happiness is in God, and serve Him in perfect fear. And furthermore, I do not wish you, under colour of devotion and holiness, to take delight in vain paintings and carvings, or in gowns embroidered with birds and beasts and flowers and other ornaments. Let those have such array, who, having only a little joy in their souls, or even none, seek all their joy in the things around them.

V

THE WEDDING GARMENT

As holy writ says: 'All the joy of a king's daughter should be within.'[9] Therefore, if you are the King of heaven's daughter—and you are if you have married His Son—be sure to hear the voice of your Father which tells you that all your joy should be within you. Make sure, then, that all your gladness comes from the spotlessness of a clean conscience in your soul. Let your soul be decked with the beautiful paintings and carvings of many virtues. Let the fresh colours of the embroideries of good habits be joined with skilful knots, so that the beauty of one virtue may make another one more bright and shining when they are both worked together.

If you let meekness be joined to chastity, nothing shall be brighter. Let simplicity be coupled with holy wisdom, and no light shall shine more clearly. Let mercy be allied with righteousness, and no honey shall be more sweet. And to all these then add good temper and good discretion, and you will never find a more valuable painting. Occupy the eyes of your heart in searching for these things; give all your strength to forming this pattern in your soul, and then the embroidery of your spiritual clothing can be stitched. And if you add, as the Book says, golden hems to this garment of many virtues, you will certainly have a dress which covers you to your very feet, and in which Christ will love to see you clothed. A hem, as you know well enough, is the last thread in a piece of cloth, of which it forms the end, and the end at which the perfection of God's law aims is charity,[10] as the apostle says. This charity you must have, loving God and your fellow Christians with a clean heart, a good conscience, and a faith unfeigned and unfailing.

In this embroidered garment, sister, find joy and happiness within your soul, and not in the things around you. Desire with all your heart true virtues, and the beauty of that kind of finery that really matters. Let your altar be covered with finest linen cloths, if such you have, for these by their whiteness and cleanness will signify and show you the whiteness of chastity and simplicity. Think how much labour and beating flax needs to change it from its earthen colour, before it is white enough to decorate your altar, and to wrap Christ's body in. At first, flax comes from the earth in an earthen colour, just as we come from our mother's womb in the wickedness of sin. 'For behold, I was conceived in iniquities, and in sins did my mother conceive me',[11] as the psalmist says. Afterwards when flax is taken from the earth, it is cast into water. So too, when we are taken from our mother's womb, we are immersed in the waters of baptism, and in them we are buried with Christ. Although sin is cast out of our souls, the sickness of sin still lasts. In baptism we are made more pure by the washing away of the filth of sin, but we are not made perfectly white and clean, for the inclination to sin and to evil remains with us as long as we are in the world.

Furthermore, after being in water, flax is dried. Similarly, after we have been christened, our body must be dried by abstinence of its inclination to uncleanness. And just as afterwards, flax is beaten with a mallet to make it more pliable to work, so our flesh too is beaten with many temptations of various kinds so as to make it more obedient to the spirit. After this, flax or linen is cleaned with large iron combs to take out the large knots and superfluous strands. And we too must put away all the things that are unnecessary with the help of the sharp pricks of discipline, keeping only what is absolutely essential. And just as afterwards a comb with smaller teeth is drawn through the flax to clean it more thoroughly, so we, when we have overcome by great efforts the wicked temptations and passions of the flesh, are cleansed of our daily faults by humble confession and due satisfaction. Next, flax is spun out in lengths: and this shows us that we too may endure in our good purpose if we persevere. And finally, just as linen is again submitted to water and fire before it is perfectly clean and white, so we are submitted to the fire of tribulation and the water of contrition before we come at last to the peace and rest of cleanness and chastity. Let the cloths of your oratory altar bring these things to your mind, so that your eyes may gaze on no hateful trifles and vanities.

VI

LOVE OF GOD AND LOVE OF MEN

As regards holy images, have on your altar the image of the Crucified hanging on the cross, which will show you the passion of Christ which you must follow. His arms are spread wide apart, so that He can clasp you more easily, and in His embrace you will find delight indeed. His breast is naked before you, to give you the milk of spiritual solace and comfort. And if you wish to praise the great excellence of virginity, have the image of the blessed maiden and mother on one side of the cross, and the dear disciple John on the other, for he was a virgin also. Thus you may be reminded how pleasant chastity is to God, both in men and in women, for He hallowed chastity in His mother and in His most loved disciple.

For that reason He joined them so tenderly together as He hung on the cross, giving the disciple to His mother, and telling the virgin disciple to take care of the mother and maiden.[12] And this was a holy legacy to Saint John, for to him, by so great an authority, was given the fairness of all mankind, hope of all the world, joy of heaven and refuge of sinners, solace of the sorrowful and comfort of the poor, and lastly lady of all the world and queen of heaven. Sister, let these things stir you to the fervour of perfect charity, and not to any thought of vanity. For at the cross, all that is necessary is that you strive for one thing alone—for one thing alone is necessary. This is that which is not found but in One, at One, and with One, in Whom there is no instability nor change. And whoever cleaves to this One is one in spirit with Him, always going on to the One Who is evermore One, without any change or failing in time.[13] This cleaving to One is charity, which, as I said, is like a golden hem which finally makes your wedding garment fair.

This wedding garment, which is skilfully interwoven with various virtues, must be trimmed about with a golden hem. This golden hem is the brightness of charity, which binds all virtues into one, sharing her beauty with them all, and making one out of many. This charity is divided into the love of God and the love of your fellow Christians. And furthermore, the love of your fellow Christians is divided into two, namely innocence and well-doing. This means that you should not grieve nor harm any man, but do good or profit to as many as you may. For this is the law of kindness: 'As you would that men should do to you, do you to them likewise'[14]—and this is well-doing. Likewise, that which you would not have done to you, do not do to another—and this is innocence.

Now take notice, sister, how these two affect you. Firstly, you should grieve no one; and surely, that ought to be easy enough for you, for you could not grieve anybody even if you wished to, unless it were by lashing him with your tongue. Then if you keep in mind the aim and purpose of your life, and love the naked and bare poverty that you have adopted, you will have no reason for evil will against any man. Covetousness has no place where nothing is loved that may be taken away. Therefore will well to all men, and do good to as many as you may. But here, no doubt, you will ask me how you can do good to any man, since you have forsaken all worldly goods and have nothing at all to give to the needy.

VII

MARTHA AND MARY: ACTION AND CONTEMPLATION

SISTER, know well the condition and calling of your life. There were once two sisters, Martha and Mary. One of them worked and the other rested. This one gave, while the other one asked and bade.[15] Martha gave outward service, and Mary nourished inward love. Mary did not run hither and thither, busy to receive guests, nor was her mind occupied with the house work, nor did she listen to the crying of poor men. But she sat meekly at the feet of Jesus, and heard devoutly His word and His sayings. My dear sister, this is your calling in life. You, who are dead to the world, must be deaf to hear anything of the world and dumb to speak it. And you must not be busy or distracted with worldly occupations. Leave Martha to these things, for although I do not deny that they are good, Mary's life is better. Lord, had Mary any feelings of envy towards Martha? Surely not: it was rather that Martha envied Mary's lot. And in the same way, let those who are high and noble women in the world be envious to follow your way of life, but you must not be envious to live as they do. It is the duty of those who live in the world to give alms if they have any worldly possessions. And it is also the duty of the men in holy church, to whom the dispensing of the church's goods is entrusted. For the things that are given to the church should be given to the poor, after the bishops, priests and clerks have taken what they need. For the goods that are given to the church are also the goods of poor men, and of widows, and of fatherless and motherless children, as well as belonging to those who administer the goods of holy church. Those who minister at the altar, rightly live by the altar. But those who receive their livelihood from the church should, in time of need, give alms and solace of what they receive, and should not shut up their money covetously in coffers.

It is reasonable also that the goods given to holy monasteries for the use of Christ's servants, should be administered by certain persons appointed by the abbot to perform this task. In this way, whatever is left after the brethren have been provided with what they need, may well be given to the guests, pilgrims and poor men, for it should not be hoarded avariciously in their own purses. But, sister, this concerns those who perform Martha's duties, and not those who rest in the holiness of contemplation as you do. For those who are in cloisters should not busy themselves with entertaining guests, nor should they have to worry with ministering to poor men, for they are those precisely who should make no provision from one day to the next, and who should give no thought nor care to meat or drink. For surely, they should be occupied with sweeter things, and taken up more profitably with spiritual delights. Let those who do not care so much for the things of the spirit, let them, I say, busy themselves with the things of the world. For there are some who are not so avid and desirous of spiritual things, just like the sinful people in the desert who were scornful of the meat of angels. Such people, when they become dulled in their own way of life, and see others occupied with temporal goods in the world, gradually become envious and start to complain, and backbite their brethren. And therefore, sister, since those who are in holy monasteries should not occupy themselves with the world —except those to whom Martha's business is assigned—all the more shall you, who have forsaken the world, have no worldly goods in your charge or possession.

You who have forsaken all, for what reason should you give alms? Nevertheless, if you have earned even a mite by your own labours, and have more than you need for your necessities, give alms of at least half of your earnings—and yet not by your own hand, but by the hand of another. Since your means of livelihood come from other people's generosity, how can you possibly give alms of the goods of other men? But you may not take for yourself more than you really need. As I said before, when I spoke of beneficence or well-doing, what alms shall you give or what good works shall you do for your fellow christians? Dear sister, a holy saint says that there is nothing richer than a good will. Then give your good will! What is more profitable than devout prayer? Give that! What is more full of humanity than pity? Spread that about! And in this way, sister, bind all the world together in your bosom with a bond of pity and of love. And there behold all good men and thank God for them. And behold, on the other hand, all those who are evil-doers and in deadly sin, and weep upon them and be sorry for their misfortune. See those too who are oppressed and weighed down by great unhappiness and calamities, and have compassion on them. Think of the hardships of the poor, the weeping of fatherless and motherless children, the desolation of widows, the bitter sighing and wailing of those who are overcome by great sorrow. Think of the needs of pilgrims, the perils of those at sea, the strict vows of holy virgins, the temptations of monks, the business of prelates, the toil of those that labour.

To all these open your heart; to all these give your alms. For these offer your bitter tears. For these pour out your pure prayers. For truly, sister, these alms are more pleasant to God, more acceptable to Christ, more in keeping with your profession, more fruitful to those to whom you give them, than any other bodily gift. And this kind of gift, that is to say, spiritual alms and spiritual well-doing, helps you in your way of life, and in no way hinders you. It increases the love of your fellow christians, and it keeps peace and tranquillity in your heart. What more shall I say? Certainly, as Saint Gregory says, there have been holy men who, in order to love God and their fellow christians more perfectly, have striven to have absolutely nothing in this world, or at least to possess what they have without covetousness. But others, in order to fulfil the law of charity, have toiled night and day to gain worldly goods so that they might give them to those in need. Yet it is to the former, and not to the latter, that Saint Gregory ascribes the perfection of charity.

VIII

MEDITATION ON THINGS PAST: FROM THE ANNUNCIATION TO THE NATIVITY

Now that I have told you something about the love of your fellow christians, I shall tell you a little briefly about the love of God. For although both of the sisters of whom I spoke loved God and their fellow christians, yet Martha was occupied more specially about the love of her fellow christians, while Mary was possessed continually by a holy affection for the everlasting and never drying well of love. Two things belong particularly to this love of God. These two are clean affection of heart, and its effect, namely, the holy conduct of life. Your affection must come from tasting spiritual sweetness, and its effect must be found in the exercise of virtues, that is to say, in a good manner of living, in fasting, in vigils, in work, in reading, in prayers, in poverty, and in other such things. And as for affection, both spiritual and bodily, you must nourish it with holy and wholesome meditation.

On this account, dear sister, so that the tender affection of love for our sweet Jesus may grow in your heart, you must have three sorts of meditation. These three are on things past, on things present, and on things to come. And therefore, sister, when your heart is cleansed of foul thoughts by the exercise of virtues, cast back your clear thoughts to those things past of which we are reminded in the true gospel.

First go to your most inward cell with Our Lady Mary, where she awaited the angel's message; and here, sister, do you also await the angel's coming, so that you may see him when he comes in, and notice how graciously and courteously he greets this gracious maid. And with your whole soul overcome by awe and praise, cry out as loud as you can when the angel begins his salutation to this blessed maid and mother, and say: Hail, Mary, full of grace, the Lord is with thee![16] Blessed art thou among women, and blessed is the fruit of thy womb, Jesus![17] And saying this over and over again, think how full and welling was the grace in Mary, for from her all this world borrowed and begged grace when God's Son was made man, full of grace and truth. Then, sister, wonder greatly in your heart how this Lord Who made heaven and earth out of nothing was enclosed within the womb of a small gentle maiden, whom God the Father hallowed, whom God the Son had as His mother, and whom God the Holy Ghost filled with grace. Ah, sweet blessed Lady, with how much grace thou wast visited, with how burning a fire of love thou wast inflamed, when thou didst feel in thy heart and in thy womb the presence of so great a majesty! For Christ took flesh of thy flesh, and of thy clean maidenly blood He made His blood, and of thy members He made His members in which dwelt the fulness of the Godhead bodily. And all this He did for you, sister, who are a maiden, so that you might love this maid and mother, and her Son, Christ, to Whom you are wedded.

Now after this, go up with your Lady to the hill where Elizabeth and the blessed Mary met together with many a sweet embrace.[18] And here watch carefully, sister, how John the Baptist hopped for joy in his mother's womb. See how he knew and saluted his Lord like a servant, his King like a knight, and the fount of all righteousness as a crier salutes a judge. And blessed were those wombs, and blessed shall they always be, from which the salvation of the world sprang out with mirth and joy to drive away the darkness of woe and sorrow which hitherto had reigned. And what will you do, sister? I pray you, run out with all haste to have your part in all this joy. Fall down before the feet of these blessed women, and in Mary's womb worship your husband Christ, and in Elizabeth's honour His friend Saint John.

And after this, wait until Mary goes up to Bethlehem, and run after her with meek devotion. And when she turns into the poor inn to bear her child,[19] come forward and do whatever service you can. And when the fair baby is cradled in an ox-stall, burst out into a song of gladness with Isaiah and say: 'Unto us a child is born, unto us a son is given.'[20] And then, with all reverence, clasp some part of the sweet stall where your young husband lies, and letting love overcome shame, press your lips to the tender feet of Christ, kissing them with all your heart many, many times before you cease. And when this is done, think within your soul of the coming of the shepherds, and see the hosts of angels singing and worshipping, and to their melody add your voice and sing: 'Glory to God in the highest!'[21]

IX

FROM THE FLIGHT INTO EGYPT TO OUR LORD'S MINISTRY

AND in your meditation do not forget the offering made by the three kings.[22] And when our Lady, for dread of Herod, flees into Egypt with her child in her lap, do not let her go alone but go with her, remembering the story which is told of her journey. It is said that our Lady on her way to Egypt, was taken by robbers.[23] Now the robber chief had a son, who went up to our Lady and found the sweet child lying in her lap. And there came such flames of light and brightness from His blessed face, that this robber knew well in his heart that the child was of greater majesty than any other poor man. And filled with great love, he clasped Him in his arms and kissed Him, saying devoutly: 'O Thou most blessed babe among all that ever were—when Thou comest to Thy great lordship, in case Thou see me at any mischief, help me and remember this time, for I will keep Thee and Thy mother safe from harm.' Sister, it is said that this was the same thief who hung on Christ's right side—the one who upbraided the thief who hung on Christ's left side, saying to him, as it is written in the gospel: 'Neither do you fear God, seeing that you are under the same condemnation. And we indeed justly, for we have received the due reward for our deeds. But this man has done no evil.'[24] Then with great meekness and contrition he turned to Christ, and seeing the same shining and brightness that he had long before seen in His face when He lay in His mother's lap, with all his heart the thief cried: 'Lord, have mind of me when Thou comest into Thy kingdom.'[25] And truly Christ did not forget His promise, for presently He answered: 'Amen I say to you, this day you will be with Me in paradise.' Sister, so as to stir yourself to a greater tenderness of love, imagine that this tale is true.

Think also how your young husband Christ, while He was a child, would play happily with the other children at Nazareth. Think too how helpful He was to His mother, and how sweet and how gracious He was to His foster father. And, sister, when He is twelve years old and goes to the temple at Jerusalem with His father and mother, and leaves them and remains behind in the city, what sorrow you will have if you seek Him for three days! How many bitter tears will run out of your eyes when you think of the sorrow of His mother Mary when she had lost so dear a child! And after, when she had found Him, with what sorrow she chided Him with this mournful reproach: 'Son, why hast

Thou done so to us? Behold Thy father and I have sought Thee sorrowing.'[26] And furthermore, if you follow this maid and mother wherever she goes, you may look for even greater confidences. And then at the River Jordan you may hear the Father's voice, and see the Son in the flesh of a man, and see the Holy Ghost in the likeness of a dove. And at this spiritual bridal feast, sister, may you receive your husband as a gift from the Father. Purification you will receive as your wedding gift from the Son; and from the Holy Ghost, the bond of love.

After this, your spouse Christ goes into the desert,[27] and stays there for many days, setting an example to the world with all its pomp and boasting. There He fasted for forty days and was tempted by the devil, thus teaching us poor wretches what battles and conflicts we must fight against the enemy of our souls. I pray you, take good heed how these things were done for you, that you may do the same.

Let there come also into your mind the unhappy woman who was taken in adultery, as the gospel relates, and remember what Jesus did and what He said when He was asked to pass judgment on her. First He wrote in the earth—and by doing this He showed that they were earthly who had accused her. And then He said: 'He that is without sin among you, let him first cast a stone at her.'[28] When this sentence had struck them all, and had driven them out of the temple, think with what piteous and godly eyes Christ looked upon her, and with how soft and sweet a voice He absolved her. Do you not think that He sighed or that He wept when He said: 'Neither will I condemn you'? And if I may make so bold as to say this, blessed was this woman who was found in adultery, and absolved by Christ from her past sins, and made secure in grace for evermore. Good Jesus, when Thou sayest, 'Neither will I condemn you', who then may condemn? When God justifies, who may accuse? But nevertheless, so that no man may be too bold because of this, let the words of Christ be heard that follow in the gospel: 'Go, and now sin no more.'

Then after this, go into the house of Simon the Pharisee, and see how the God-man Christ sits there at meat.[29] And steal out with that blessed sinner Mary Magdalene, and wash Christ's feet with your hot tears, and wipe them with the hairs of your head. Gaze softly on Him, and at last anoint Him with spiritual ointment. Lord, sister, will not your soul be pervaded through and through by this precious perfume? But in case, because of your unworthiness, your husband Christ draws away His feet and will not allow you to kiss them, you must nevertheless stand there and pray meekly. Set your eyes on Him, full though they are with tears, and with deep sighs and piteous crying attract the attention of Him Whom you desire with all your heart. Wrestle earnestly with your God, as Jacob did, for He will be glad when you overcome Him. And perhaps it will seem to you at some time that He takes His gaze off you; that He closes His ears and will not hear you, and that He hides His feet so that you may not kiss them. But in spite of all this, make sure that you still stand in front of Him, and cry out loudly to Him without ceasing: 'How long dost Thou turn away Thy face from me? Restore to me, good Jesus, the joy of Thy salvation. For my heart has said to Thee: My face has sought Thee. Thy face, O Lord, will I seek.'[30] And, if I may be so bold as to say this, He will hardly deny His feet to you who are a maiden, when He granted them to be kissed by a sinful woman.

And you must see that you do not forget that house where the man smitten with the palsy was let down through the tiles before the feet of Jesus, and where pity and power met together. 'Son,' said Christ, 'your sins are forgiven you.'[31] Ah Jesus, Thy wonderful pity, Thy mercy may not be spoken of! This blessed man had remission of his sins, which outwardly he had not confessed, and which no contrition nor satisfaction had merited. He asked for health for his body, and the merciful Christ granted him health both of body and soul. Now surely, good God, life and death are in Thy hands. And if Thy will is to save me, no man may forbid it. But if Thou wilt finally damn me, no man may be so bold as to ask why Thou doest so. If the envious Pharisee begrudges that Christ is so merciful as to forgive a simple man his sins, presently Christ answers: 'Is it not lawful for me to do what I will? Is your eye evil because I am good?'[32] For surely, Christ will have mercy on whom He wishes, despite the Pharisee's scornful gaze.

And therefore let us weep and cry and pray that it may be Christ's will to save us and have mercy on us. And so that our prayer may be the more efficacious, let it be confirmed with good deeds and in that way let our devotion be increased, and the burning love in our souls be stirred to God. In our prayers, let us lift up our clean hands, which no blood of sin has defiled, no unclean touching has stained, and no avarice has estranged. And let our heart be lifted up without anger and without strife, now that tranquillity has set it at rest, and peace has made it fair, and cleanness of conscience has made it full of life and vigour. We do not read that the man with the palsy had any of these things, but nevertheless he got full remission of his sins. Assuredly this shows us the wonderful power of the great mercy of God; and although it would be blasphemy to deny God's mercy, yet it is presumption to base all our hopes on it. For of this there is no doubt—God may say to whomsoever He wishes what He said to the man with the palsy, 'Son, your sins are forgiven you'. But whoever rests in the hope that these words will be said to him without his own efforts, without deep contrition, without sincere confession and prayers of repentance—without fail, his sins shall never be forgiven him.

X

HOLY THURSDAY

But now, sister, let us go to Bethany, to the blessed feast of Jesus, Martha, Mary and Lazarus, where the blessed bonds of love and friendship were made sacred by the authority of Christ. The gospel says: 'Jesus loved Martha, and her sister Mary, and Lazarus',[33] and no one doubts that this refers to the great privilege of a very special love which Jesus had for all of them. And indeed Jesus did love them fervently: and we have an ample witness to this in the sweet and tender tears that He wept with them for Lazarus when he was dead. And all the people around understood that this was a sign of special love, for they said: 'Behold how He loved him.'

But let us now speak of the great feast that these three made for Jesus, as the gospel tells us. Martha served, Lazarus was one of them that sat at meat, and Mary Magdalene took an alabaster box of precious ointment, and breaking the box, she poured the ointment on Jesus' head.[34] Sister, be glad with all your heart that you are at this feast, and notice carefully, I pray you, what each person does and says. Martha ministers to the needs of those who sit at table, Lazarus sits in Our Lord's company, and Mary anoints the head of Jesus. Dear sister, this last thing is your duty. Therefore break the alabaster box of your heart, and all that you ever have had, or might have, of devotion, of love, of affection, of holy desires, of any kind of spiritual sweetness —pour it altogether on the head of your spouse, and worship the true God in the form of a man, and a true man Who is also God. And although Judas the traitor may gnash his teeth at you and complain; although he may be envious of you and scorn you, and say that this ointment of spiritual devotion is only wasted, take no notice of him. 'Why was this waste of the ointment made? It might have been sold for three hundred pence and given to the poor!'[35] These are the words of many men nowadays. But why? The Pharisee groused, because he envied Mary's penance. Judas complained, because he was filled with envious desires for the precious ointment. But truly, He Who was a rightful and merciful judge, He would have none of these accusations. She whom they accused, Christ absolved and excused. 'Suffer her to do so,' He says, 'for she has done a good deed to me.'

Let Martha therefore work at the task around her, and busy herself in ministering to those about her. Let her receive pilgrims, give meat to the hungry and drink to the thirsty, and clothing to the naked, and so on. But let Mary's part be enough for me, and I will look to none but her. Who indeed would advise me to leave the feet of Jesus, which Mary kissed so sweetly? Or to turn away my eyes from that blessed face, so fair and so fresh, that Mary looked at so undistractedly? Or else to close my ears to those sweet words of Christ on which Mary fed with such satisfaction?

And now, sister, let us arise and leave this place. But where are we going, you ask? Surely we are leaving this place so that you may follow your meek husband, Who is the Lord of heaven and earth, as He sits upon an ass. And in your astonishment at the great honour and reverence that is done Him as He sits there, summon all your strength and cry out with the children of the Hebrews who worship Him so devoutly: 'Hosanna, blessed is He that comes in the name of the Lord.'[36] And then make your way into that beautiful large hall, freshly strewn with reeds and prepared for Christ's supper on Holy Thursday, and thank God that you may come to such a feast. Let love overcome all your shame, let steadfast affection exclude all dread and awe, and pray that you may have a few alms of the crumbs from that blessed table. Or else, sister, stand afar off, and like a poor wretch gazing upon a great lord, stretch out your hand so that He may have pity on your hunger.

And when Christ rises up from supper, and girds Himself about with a linen cloth, and puts water into a basin,[37] think how wonderful is that majesty of God that washes and wipes so carefully the feet of sinful men, and how great an act of love and kindness it is to handle with His holy hands the feet of Judas, His cursed traitor. Dwell and think on these things, sister, and with much devotion put forth your own feet last of all to be washed as others' are. For be sure of this, that he who is not washed and made clean by Him, can have no part with Him in the bliss of paradise. Sister, are you in a hurry to leave this place? Stay a while, I beg you, and look well at him who leans with so much boldness on Christ's breast, and rests with so much favour on His lap.[38] Blessed is that man, whoever he may be! Ah, now I see who it is! Without doubt, John is his name. Now good Saint John, I beg thee tell me if thou wilt, what sweetness, what grace, what light, what devotion, what goodness thou dost draw from that ever-welling fountain, Christ. Indeed, there are all the treasures of knowledge and wisdom. There is the well of mercy, the house of pity, the honey of everlasting sweetness. Ah, sweet and dear disciple, how hast thou got all this? Art thou higher than Peter, or holier than Andrew? Art thou more accepted by Christ than all the other apostles? Truly, the great privilege of thy chastity has merited all this dignity for thee; for thou wast chosen as one of God's maidens, and therefore thou art the most loved of all thy brethren. Now, sister, you are also a chaste maiden; so rejoice and draw near with all reverence, and ask for some part of all this sweet worthiness for yourself. And if you do not dare to approach further, let the chosen disciple sleep on at Christ's breast, and let him drink the priceless wine which is to be found in the knowledge of the almighty Godhead. But run, sister, to the breast of His humanity, and drink the milk from it, so that you may be fed in spirit with thoughts of what He did for us in our flesh.

XI

THE PASSION

AND at the same time, meekly bow your head so that you may hear the same prayer said for you which Christ said before His passion when He commended His disciples to the Father in these holy words: 'Holy Father, keep them in Thy name.'[39] And I know that it would be a very happy thing for you to remain here longer, but yet, sister, you must be patient. And therefore you must follow Christ, when He goes to Mount Olivet to pray in a sweat of blood. And although He takes no one with Him but Peter, James and John, and goes with them into some private and hidden place, at least you can see how our good God took our wretchedness upon Himself. Notice how He Who is the Lord of all begins, as a man, to be aghast and to say: 'My soul is sorrowful even unto death.'[40] My good Lord God, what is this? It seems that Thou hast so great a compassion for me, and that Thou lovest me so much as to become man for me, that Thou hast forgotten, as it were, that Thou art truly God. Thou fallest down on Thy face and prayest for me, and in Thine anguish Thou dost sweat so grievously that it seems like drops of blood running down on the earth.

Where are you standing, sister? Why are you still? Run, for God's sake, and drink up the sweet and blessed drops that they may not be spilled, and with your tongue lick away the dust from His feet. And if you can do no more, see that you do not fall asleep as Peter did, lest you should hear the sorrowful reproach that Christ made to Peter: 'Might you not watch one hour with Me?'

And presently, see how Judas the traitor comes up to Christ, and what a cursed company of Jews follows after him. At this treacherous traitor's kiss of guile, see how they set hands upon your Lord, and how fiercely they snatch Him and lead Him away like a thief; how cruelly they bind those sweet and tender hands with cords. Alas, who may suffer this? Sister, I know well that pity now fills all your heart, and sorrow and compassion have set your breast on fire. But nevertheless suffer awhile, sister, and let Him die for you, Who wishes to die for us all. Do not draw any sword or stick to defend Him. Do not be filled with rash indignation. For although you would wish to cut off any man's ear, as Peter in fact did; or even if you were to strike off an arm or leg, Christ will certainly restore all this as He did Malchus' ear.[41] Yes, and although you would slay any man to avenge your husband, without doubt He will raise him from death to life. Therefore, sister, let things be as they are, and follow Him to the hall of the prince of priests where He is condemned. Do you wash with the tears of your eyes that fairest face that ever was, which the accursed Jews defiled with their foul spittle. Consider with what eyes of pity, and how sweetly and mercifully He looked upon Peter when he had forsaken Him, and how Peter, turning away, wept bitterly for his sin.[42]

Good Jesus, grant that Thy sweet eye might look once mercifully upon me who have so often in some way or another forsaken Thee by my foul thoughts and wicked deeds! But now, sister, next day your spouse Christ is taken treacherously to Pilate. There He is accused, but He holds His peace, and as a sheep that is led to death, or as a lamb to the shearing, He opens not His mouth.[43] Watch carefully how gently and courteously He stands before the judge, with His head bowed and His eyes cast down; with good cheer and few words. For your sake He is all ready to be despised, and all ready for the cruel scourging. I am sure, sister, that you cannot suffer this for long. You cannot stand there and see His comely back torn with whips, His gracious face swollen with blows, His worshipful head crowned with thorns that pierce Him to the brain, and that right hand that made heaven and earth, mocked with a reed for a sceptre. I know full well that you cannot endure for long to see these things. But yet nevertheless, you must look. And after all this, He is brought out, all blood-stained and beaten, with a crown of thorns on His head, and a purple garment on His body.

Then Pilate said to the Jews: 'Behold the man!'[44] Indeed He is a man, wretched though He is. Who doubts it? The hard beating of the sharp scourges, the livid colour of His wounds, the filth of spittle on His face, all bear ample witness to the fact that He is a man. But in case you say to me that even with all His injuries He is not angry as a man would be, that He does not take vengeance on His tormentors as a man would do, then I grant that He is more than a man. Now He is proved to be a man, as He suffers the false condemnation of evil men; but when He shall come to judge on the last day He shall then be known as a very mighty God. Now nevertheless, the false Pilate sits solemnly in the judgment seat while Jesus stands before him. And so, piteously bearing His own gallows, He is led to death. But behold, sister, this very gallows tree is a wonderful sign that your husband Christ is a prince and a most worshipful

Lord. As the Book says, 'the government shall be upon His shoulder',[45] and the cross is 'the rod of His righteousness, and the sceptre of His kingdom'.[46]

They stripped Him of His garments, and these were divided among the soldiers—all, that is, except His precious coat which Our Lady had woven without seam. It was not to be cut, so it fell intact to the lot of one of them. Then between thieves He was stretched on the cross, and His sweet hands were pierced through with nails. They offered Him a drink of wine mixed with gall, and many other despites they did to Him. And so He Who is the mediator between God and man hung between heaven and earth, bringing, as it were, heaven and earth together. Heaven is aghast, and the earth is filled with wonder. And what do you do, sister? Surely, it would be no wonder if you were sad, for the sun, a creature without reason, is sad too. If the earth trembles and quakes,[47] what wonder if you also tremble? If even hard rocks break in two, what wonder if your heart bursts apart? Since the women weep who stand beside the cross, why should anyone be surprised if you weep for sorrow at so piteous a death? But while you suffer all these things, think well of the mildness in the heart of Christ: what patience, what pity, what love and kindness He had in His heart throughout His torments! He takes no notice of His injuries. He does not consider His bitter pains. He does not accuse His enemies of the villainies and despites that are done to Him. He takes no account of all this, but He takes pity and compassion on those who torture Him in His passion. He prepares healing for those who give Him smarting wounds, and He obtains life for them while they are about to put Him to death. With what great sweetness of heart, do you think, with what mildness of all His spirit, with how great a depth of charity does He cry to the Father: 'Father, forgive them!'[48]

XII

A PRAYER AT THE PASSION

Sweet and kind Jesus, behold me here at Thy feet, a simple and devout worshipper of Thy majesty, who does not scorn Thy infirmity and weakness; an adorer of Thy piteous death; an acknowledger of Thy great mercy, and not a despiser of the suffering body that Thou hast taken from mankind. And therefore I pray and beg Thee that Thy sweet blessed manhood might pray for me, and that Thy wonderful pity might commend me to Thy Father. Sweet Jesus, say for me, who worship Thy passion and Thy death with a heart full of meekness and humility, those words which Thou didst say for them who put Thee to death. Merciful Lord, say once for me to Thy Father, 'Father, forgive him!' And you, sister, who, being a maiden, should have an even fuller and deeper love for this maiden's son Christ, leave those women who stood afar off, as the gospel says;[49] and with the mother and maiden Mary, and with Saint John, who was also a virgin, go sadly to the cross of Christ, and see how this face that angels delight to look upon, is all dim and pale. Look also to one side and see how Mary stands there, and see how her fresh maidenly face is all swollen and wet with weeping. Lord, sister, how could you stand by with dry eyes, when you see so many tears running down her fair cheeks? How could you fail to sob and weep when you see a sword of such sharp sorrow run through her tender heart? How could you hear without great feeling how Christ said to His mother: 'Woman, behold thy son'; and to Saint John: 'Behold thy mother'?

After all these things, one of the soldiers with a spear pierced His side to the tender heart.[50] And then, as the gospel says, there came out blood and water. Run, sister, run and do not delay, for His blood is turned into wine to make you drunk, and the water into milk to nourish you in your spirit. Here are fresh, fair running rivers for you. Here are His wounds, like holes in the rock which is His body, welcoming you as a dovecote welcomes the dove. Kiss each wound until your lips, like those of the bride in the Canticle, are like a scarlet lace,[51] and your words, like hers, are sweet.

But wait now, for Joseph of Arimathea, that noble man, comes to untie Christ's hands and feet, gently drawing out the nails. See how he clasps the sweet body of Christ in his arms, and how he draws it to his breast. In truth, this blessed man might well say what is written in the Canticle: 'A bundle of myrrh is my beloved to me; he shall abide between my breasts.'[52] Go after this holy man, sister, and follow the precious treasure of heaven and earth, and bear up the hand or foot that hangs down so piteously, or else gather up the drops of blood that fall down from His wounds, and lick the dust from His blessed feet. And behold how sweetly and diligently the holy man Nicodemus treats the sacred members of Christ, and anoints them with sweet ointments. See how he wraps Christ's body in a clean cloth, and together with holy Joseph lays it in the sepulchre.

XIII

THE RESURRECTION

AFTER all this, make sure that you do not quit the fellowship of Mary Magdalen; but when she goes to Christ's sepulchre with her sweet-smelling balms to anoint Christ's body,[53] follow her. Ah Lord, sister, if only you might be worthy to see with the eyes of your soul that which Mary saw with the eyes of her body . . . within the sepulchre, one angel at the head, another at the foot, singing and praising the joy and bliss of Christ's resurrection . . . Jesus looking happily on Mary Magdalen who was weeping, full of sorrow for His death . . . now His sweet voice as He calls her by name: 'Mary!'[54] What could be sweeter than this word, or more joyful and blissful—Mary! Now Mary, let thy tears run down, and thy sighs come forth. What heart didst thou have, what spirit, what strength, when thou didst fall headlong at Christ's feet, and didst greet Him saying: 'Rabboni!' I pray thee tell me, with what affection, with what burning desire of thy heart thou didst cry out, for thou couldst not say more for sobbing and weeping when thou saidst, 'Rabboni'. The great love that thou didst have for Jesus had filled all the senses of thy body and soul.

But Thou, dearest Lord, why didst Thou keep at a distance someone who loved Thee so much and so burningly, so that she might not come near enough to Thee to kiss Thy holy feet? 'Touch me not',[55] said Christ. A hard and insufferable word, a word that would break even a heart of stone. 'Touch me not.' Why, blissful Lord? Why may I not come near to Thee? Why may I not touch the dear feet that were pierced for me with nails on the cross? Why may I not handle them, nor kiss them? Good Jesus, hast Thou become a stranger to me, and no more my friend, now that Thy body is even more glorious after Thy resurrection? Now for sure, I will not let Thee go, and I will not go from Thee. I shall never cease from weeping. My breast and heart will break for sobbing and sighing unless I touch Thy feet just once. And then says the merciful Jesus: 'I am not yet ascended to my Father.' That which you ask, He says, is not taken from you but is only delayed.

'Go to my brethren, and say to them: I ascend to my Father. . . .'

Then Mary runs from the garden, and surely she runs all the faster, so that she may come back to it more quickly. And when she comes again, she does not come alone, but with other women; and Jesus Himself goes up to them, and with a loving and merry greeting He comforts those who were overcome with bitter sorrow at His death. Sister, I beg you notice how that which was at first denied is now granted to Mary Magdalen and her companions. As the gospel says: 'They went and clasped Jesus about His feet.'[56] Think about all these happenings, sister, and meditate on them often. In these things have all your delight and pleasure, and let no sleep nor outward occupation take your mind off them. But because in this life of wretchedness nothing is stable and nothing is abiding, no man dwells nor tarries in any one state of mind. Therefore our souls should be fed with all kinds of different thoughts. And so we shall now pass from the things that are past to think about the things that are present, for by these we may be stirred to a more perfect love of our God.

XIV

MEDITATION ON THINGS PRESENT: GOD'S PATIENCE WITH SINFUL MEN

It is a great gift of God, I think, if we consider those who have gone before us; how we may be kept from the many misfortunes and evil deeds in which they were involved; how God made us of the same matter as they, and yet we have not suffered the same fate as many of them. For some have been born dead from their mother's womb, and others have been born into pain rather than into life. What a cause for sorrow we should have been both to ourselves and to others if God, instead of making us sound and whole in wind and limb, had allowed us to be born with some dreadful sickness or with the palsy, or even crooked and lame. What a great goodness it was, that He ordained us to be born among those who would teach us to believe in God, for this gift is denied to many thousands. It is freely given to us, who because of His goodness are chosen through His grace. And yet we are all in the same state and condition, being all members of the human race. Think deeply on these things, and see how great a benefit of God it was that we were fed and cared for by our father and mother. And see how God has kept us so that we were not burned by fire, nor drowned, nor bitten by some poisonous snake, nor tried and tempted by the devil; nor did we fall and break our necks as many others have done. And it was also one of God's great gifts that we were taught our holy faith when we were young, and instructed in the holy sacraments of the church.

Sister, let us think well about these things. For we are both sharers in these gifts and graces, since not only do we have the same state and condition as human beings, but we were also born of the same father and mother. This is one of God's gifts to our body. But think to yourself what God has done by His grace to your soul, for there He has distinguished between you and me as light is distinguished from darkness. He has always kept you for Himself in cleanness and purity, but He has left me alone to myself. My merciful God, what have I become, whither have I strayed? I was cast out from Thy blessed presence as Cain was. I made my dwelling upon the earth—that is to say, I gave my unclean love to earthly things. I was wandering about with Cain whom Thou hadst cursed, and whoever met me had power to slay me.[57] And no wonder, for what is a wretched creature to do when he is forsaken by his creator? Where is a wandering sheep to go, or where is it to lie, when it is abandoned by its shepherd? Ah sister, have pity on me, for a wild beast has devoured your brother,[58] and that beast is the most wicked beast of all—the devil. Therefore, sister, look at me, and then look at yourself and see how much your God has done for you, for He has kept you and saved you from that wicked beast. How wretched was I, though, when I defiled myself and lost my cleanness and chastity! How blessed are you, whose chastity and purity only the grace of God has defended and kept! How often was your maidenhood assailed, tempted and stirred to rebellion, and yet it was preserved and kept by God; and I wilfully fell into many grievous sins, preparing coals of fire to burn and torture me, the stench of sin to kill me, and crawling worms to gnaw me in hell, were it not for the mercy of my God.

Good sister, think on this, for you sometimes used to weep over me and reproach me when you were only a young girl. But indeed that passage of Holy Writ is quite true where it says: 'No man may amend whom God has despised',[59] that is, without great repentance on the part of man and special grace given by God. Ah, how deeply you ought to love your good God Who, when He despised me, drew you to Himself. And although we were born of one father and mother, He hated me and loved you. Think of my foulness and corruption, for there was no one to defend me nor save me from such mischief. Wicked company had had an evil effect upon me, its sweet drink of fleshly love making me drunk with poison and foul impurity. My merciful God, Thy anger and Thy wrath fell upon me, and I did not feel them at all. I had flown far from Thee, and Thou didst allow it all. I had sunk into all kinds of filth, and yet Thou didst let me alone. See, sister, see how I ask you to take heed! For you might have fallen into the same hateful state into which my evil will cast me, had not the mercy of Christ kept you and preserved you.

But I do not say this as though I were complaining against God, nor as though He had not been good and kind and loving to me. For even without all the benefits and gifts that I have mentioned—which we both share together—the patience and the loving kindness of God were wonderfully shown to me in many ways: for while I was in deadly sin, the earth did not open to swallow me up; and I am greatly indebted to God that heaven did not strike me down with thunder and lightning, that I was not drowned, that I did not die suddenly by some horrible death. For how could any of God's creatures put up with the terrible wrongs that I had done to the Creator, unless God Himself restrained them?

XV

GOD'S MERCY, GRACE AND GOODNESS

BUT God desires neither the death nor the damnation of any sinful wretch, but wishes rather that he should turn from his wickedness and live his life in grace. And what a great gift of mercy and grace and goodness was it that, when I ran away from Him, my God pursued after me to draw me back to Himself again? When I was in deadly fear of everlasting damnation, He comforted me and gave me life. When I was cast down into the depths of despair, He lifted me up again in perfect hope. And when I was most estranged from Him, He came to me with His great benefits to stir me to turn to Him again.

And when I was altogether used to the uncleanness and filth of sin, He drew me away from it with the savour and taste of spiritual sweetness in my soul, and He broke the strong chains and bonds of my evil habits. And afterwards, when I had left the world for the cloister, He received me lovingly to His grace. I do not mention many of the wonderful and great benefits and gifts that His mercy has bestowed on me, so that I may take no part of that praise which is altogether His. For in many men's thought, the goodness and the graciousness of him who gives and the fortune and prosperity of him who receives are so closely linked, that he who receives is praised as well as he who gives; and that is wrong. For what goodness has any wretched man, but what he has received as a gift from God? And therefore, my dearest Lord, to Thee alone be worship, to Thee be praise, to Thee be joy, to Thee be all the thanks that pure hearts can utter! But for me, a sinful wretch, let there be nothing but confusion and shame, for I have done many evil things after having received many graces and much goodness. But you may perhaps ask me, sister, in what way I have less than you of God's grace. Ah, now, answer me this: who is the more fortunate—the one who, with fair and easy weather, brings his ship to the harbour safe and sound, and full of riches and merchandise; or he who, when his ship has been broken in the wild waves and roaring storms, only escapes to land barely alive, naked and trembling?

Sister, you have every reason to be glad and to rejoice at these great riches, the gifts of the grace of God that has kept you free from the tempest of deadly temptation. But with great toil and labour I must make whole again that which was broken, find again that which was lost, and piece together again that which was torn in the tempest of temptation. And nevertheless, you must realize that you ought to be ashamed, sister, if I am found equal to you in the life to come, after I have committed so many hateful deeds in my life on earth. And yet it often happens that many different sins and vices take away the reward and happiness of maidenhood; while, on the other hand, the change from an evil life, and the virtues that follow upon vices, wipe away the stain and shame of former evil ways.

And now, sister, look upon the great gift of the goodness of God that you have received, as you know full well. With what cheer He came to you, when you left the world to come to Him! With what wonderful delights He fed you when you were hungering for Him! What riches of His mercy He bestowed upon you; what holy desires He inspired in your soul, and what a sweet drink of charity He gave you! For if God in His great and merciful love and kindness has not left me, a fugitive from His judgment and a rebel from His law, without some slight experience of His wonderful spiritual comforts—what wonderful sweetness He must have given to you who are, and always were, a chaste and pure maiden! If you have ever been in temptation, He has defended you. If you have been in peril and danger, He has kept you safe. If you have been in sorrow, He has comforted and strengthened you. If your mind was filled with doubts, He has set your thoughts aright. How often, sister, when you have been sad, or dull, or weary of your way of life, has He been a merciful comfort to you? How often, when you have longed and burned for love of Him, has He leaped into your heart? How often, when you have been reading and studying Holy Scripture, has He enlightened your soul with the light of spiritual understanding? How often, when you have been at prayer, has He inspired you to such great desires that you could not even mention them to anyone? How often has He withdrawn your heart from all worldly things, and taken it up to the delights of heaven and the joy of paradise? Think of all this in your heart, so that all your affection and all your love may be turned to Him alone. Have only scorn for all the world, and let all fleshly love be as nothing to you. Do you, who have given over your whole life to God and to those who are in heaven and live with God, think that you are no longer in this world. For where your treasure is, let your heart be also.

Be sure that you do not shut your soul up in a purse full of silver and gold and worldly riches, for your soul will never be able to fly up easily to the joy and happiness of heaven if it is burdened with even so much as a pennyweight. If you were to imagine yourself as dying every day, you would have no care for tomorrow and what it would bring. Let there be no imaginable trouble in the days to come that could make you afraid, but let all your trust and hope be in Him Who feeds the birds of the air, and arrays the lilies and flowers of the field with more beauty than Solomon ever had in all his finery.[60] Let Him be your storehouse; let Him be your gold purse, your riches and all your delight and pleasure. Let Him be everything to you in all your needs, Who is blessed for ever and ever, amen. This is enough, I think, sister, for our meditation on things present.

XVI

MEDITATION ON THINGS TO COME: THE THOUGHT OF JUDGMENT

WHAT great gifts are kept for us in the life to come by Him, Who grants such great benefits to His servants in this world? The beginning of things that are to come, and the end of things that are now, is death. And who is there, or what is there, that has no horror of death? What heart does not dread it? Beasts and birds are very careful to avoid death, and defend their lives by swift running, and by hiding in their lairs, and in many other ways. Sister, you must search your own soul to see what your conscience answers you on this matter, what your faith believes, what your hope promises you, and what your desire yearns for. If life is drudgery for you, and if you are sad and despise the world and your own flesh, then indeed you long for death with a great desire. For death rids us of the drudgery of this life, and puts an end to sadness in this world, and frees the body from much sorrow.

One thing that is worth more than all the delights and pleasures of this world, is with a clean conscience and sure hope to be free from the fear of the death of your body. And surely, sister, if you have no dread of death, this is the joyful beginning of the everlasting bliss that is to come, and a pledge of happiness that God will fulfil in paradise. And when death comes, and your last hours on earth run short, your perfect faith will overcome your natural horror, while hope will temper it, and the certainty you feel by reason of your pure conscience will put away all dread. See, sister, how death is the beginning of rest and of bliss, the end of toil and labour, and the flight from vice and wretchedness. As the Book says: 'Blessed are they who die in the Lord.'[61] And it was because this saying is true that the prophet, distinguishing between the death of those who are beloved of God and the death of those who are accursed and shall be damned, said: 'All glorious kings died in joy.'[62] For they die in great joy and gladness, whose death is commended by a pure and perfect conscience. Their death is very precious indeed in the sight of God.[63] And in truth a man at whose death angels are present is a glorious king, and he dies in great joy. At his last sleep the saints come and give help to their new fellow citizen of heaven. They give him comfort and strength, and fight for him against his enemies; they cast down those who withstand him, and convict his accusers, leading his soul to Abraham's bosom and to the light of God, where he will abide in rest, peace and light.

But it is not thus for those whom God has cursed, for to them the same prophet says: 'You are cast out of your sepulchre (that is, out of your body) as an unthrifty dry stick that is worthless, except for the fire.'[64] For those whom God has cursed are drawn at their death by wicked spirits out of their bodies, which are all defiled with lechery and covetousness. And with hellish instruments of torture they are dragged to be burned in the fire and gnawed by worms. Now it is rightly said that the hope of righteous men is the joy and bliss of heaven, while the hope of wicked men shall perish and fail. But what rest, what peace, what mirth and light are promised and kept for the blessed spirits that rest in Abraham's bosom! Experience has not yet taught me what these rewards are like, and so no pen of mine ought to write about it as I think it is. But the saints wait in the bliss of paradise until the number of their brethren is completed on the day of the last resurrection and judgment. And then they shall be clothed in a double stole,[65] that is to say, in the joy of body and soul together, in the happiness of heaven that never ends.

XVII

DOOMSDAY

I BEG you, sister, to think about the joy and horror of that day of doom. When the angels of heaven shall be, as it were astonished; when the elements shall be dissolved in the heat of fire, then hell's gates shall be opened, and all that is now hidden from us shall be known. From above shall come the judge, in strength and anger: His wrath shall burn like fire, and His chariot shall be as terrible as a roaring tempest when He takes His vengeance in His terrible anger, and destroys His enemies in a flame of lightning. Now indeed that man is blessed who is ready to meet his judge at that time. What sorrow shall those wretches feel who now defile themselves with lechery, who put their minds into a turmoil with covetousness, and are conceited with the pride of Lucifer? Angels shall fly and separate the wicked from the good, putting righteous men on God's right side, and on His left side those that shall be damned. Sister, imagine now within your heart that you are between these two sides, before the judgment seat of God, and not yet sent either to left or to right. Look to the left of this rightful judge, Christ, and gaze upon the cursed, wretched and sorry throng. Ah sister, what horror, what dread, what sorrow, what a stench of sin! The damned men who stand there look like dwarfs, and they gnash their teeth as they wait there with their faces deformed by sin—a horrible sight—with their bodies naked and foul. They would dearly like to hide themselves, but they may not do so. If they lift up their gaze, they see nothing but the wrath and anger of their dreadful judge. If they look down, the pit of hell with all its horrors yawns at their feet. They can find no excuses for their sins, and they cannot appeal against any unjust judgment; for whatever the Almighty Judge decides, their own consciences tell them that it is right.

Think, sister, how you ought to love Him with all your might, Who has kept you from that unhappy crowd, and has clasped you in His grace, and has purified you and justified you, so as to bring you to eternal bliss with Him. Therefore gaze over towards His right side, and see the happy company in which He has placed you. Ah Jesus, what beauty is theirs, what honour, what happiness! What joy, what security they feel in Him! Some are raised on high to be made sharers of the judgment seat of Christ. Some are shining brightly with the crown of martyrdom. Some are as white as the lily of virginity. Some are laden with the fruit of alms-giving. Some shine with a pure and unmarred light that shines from their knowledge of God's teaching and law. The sweet face of Jesus looks down on them in all its brightness, and it is full of love and happiness, sweetness and comfort, making them glad in Him; while on those whom He has cursed, His face looks down in anger and judgment.

If you were to stand, sister, between these two throngs, waiting to know to which side you would be condemned, you would be able to say with the psalmist: 'Fear and trembling have come upon me, and darkness has covered me.'[66] Lord, how hard it would be for you to wait there. For if He were to put you on the left side, you would not be able to say that He was unjust. If He sent you to the right side, it would be solely because of His grace, and not because of any merits of your own. Indeed, good Lord, life and death depend on Thy will and on Thy power alone. Do you see now, sister, how all your heart and all your soul should be fixed only on the love of Him? Although He might well give you the same sentence of death as He will give to those that are damned, yet in His goodness He would rather put you on His right side and include you among those whom He loves. And therefore imagine that you are already in that holy company, and that you can hear the decree that His lips utter: 'Come, you blessed of my Father, receive the kingdom that was made ready for you before the beginning of the world.'[67] And then shall the sorry wretches hear the hard and unutterable sentence pronounced:

'Depart from me, you cursed, into everlasting fire.' And then these will go into perpetual torment, while righteous men go into the happiness that will never end. Ah, it is a sad and hard journey, a wretched and pitiful state for those who are condemned to the captivity of hell. And when they are taken away and separated completely from the bliss of God, and the righteous men are placed among the angels according to their merits—let the glorious procession go into the high Jerusalem, the everlasting city of heaven. Christ Himself will be at its head, and all the members of His body that are gathered together in Him shall follow in His train.

XVIII

THE KINGDOM OF ETERNAL BLISS

THERE the glorious King shall reign in them, and they in Him. And they shall receive the kingdom of eternal bliss as their inheritance that was prepared for them even before the world was created. We cannot know what that kingdom will be like, and so how can we write about it? But this I know for sure, and I make so bold as to say—that you will lack nothing that you desire, and you will not have anything that you would rather be without. There shall be no weeping nor wailing, no sorrow nor dread, no discord nor envy, no tribulation nor temptation. There will be no such thing as corruption, suspicion or ambition; no such thing as the sickness of old age, death or poverty; no trace of need or weariness or faintness. And where none of these things is to be found, what else may there be but perfect joy and mirth and peace; perfect security, and unmarred love and charity; perfect riches, beauty and rest; health and strength and the perfect sight of God? And in that everlasting and perpetual life what more could you want? God our creator will be clearly seen, known and loved. He will be seen in Himself as He reigns in perfect bliss. He will be seen in His creatures as He governs and rules all things without the least trouble or toil, as He keeps all things unwearyingly, and as He gives Himself to all things in the measure that they can receive Him, without any lessening of His Godhead. The face of God that the angels desire to gaze upon, shall be seen in all its sweetness, lovableness and desirability. But who may speak of the clearness and brightness of that vision?

There shall we see the Father in the Son, the Son in the Father, and the Holy Ghost in Them both. There God our creator will be seen, not as in a mirror or in darkness, but face to face, as the gospel says. There God will be seen as He is, when the promise that He made in the gospel is fulfilled: 'Who loves Me shall be loved by My Father, and I shall love him and show him My own self.'[68] And it is from this clear sight of Him that that blissful knowledge comes of which Christ speaks in the gospel: 'This is eternal life, that they may know Thee, the one true God, and Jesus Christ Whom Thou didst send.'[69] From this knowledge there springs so great a fervour of blissful desire, so much fullness of love, so much sweetness of charity, that the completeness of bliss may not take away the joyful desire, nor may the desire stand in the way of completeness. And how can we say all this in a few words? Surely, sister, it is in this way: 'Eye has not seen, nor ear heard, what God has made ready for those who love Him.'[70]

Now, sister, I have written a few words to you about the memory of Christ's benefits that are in the past, and about the experience of those that are present, and of the lasting hope of those that are to come. And this I have done so that a more plenteous fruit of the love of God may spring out of your heart. These three ways of meditation will stir the love and affection of your spirit. Your affection will give birth to a burning desire, and your desire will lead you to sigh and weep for the love of your husband Christ, until you are brought into His sight and clasped in His blessed arms. Then you may say to your only love what is written in holy writ in the book of love: 'My beloved is mine, and I am his.'[71]

And so now you have what you wanted and asked from me. I have given you information concerning the body, so that you may be able to rule and govern the outward man. I have given you also a way of purifying the inward man of vices, so as to make him beautiful in virtue. And I have shown you in a threefold meditation, how you must nourish your soul and stir yourself to the love of God. And in case any devout soul profits from reading this little book, I beg him to do me this favour—to pray devoutly for my misdeeds to my Saviour for Whom I wait, and to my Judge Whom I dread; and to beg God that he and I may both come to that bliss of heaven of which I have spoken so unworthily. And may He grant this Who lives and reigns for ever and ever. Amen.

NOTES

[1] 1 Corinthians vii. 34.
[2] St. Matthew xix. 12.
[3] Proverbs iii. 16.
[4] Ecclesiasticus xxxiv. 9 (LXX)
[5] Revelation xiv. 4.
[6] Although this quotation is eminently suitable for the story of Saint Agnes, it comes in fact from the fourth lesson of the feast of Saint Cecilia (Matins, November 22nd).
[7] Genesis xxxii. 26.
[8] 1 Corinthians i. 31.
[9] Psalm xliv. 14 (Vulgate).
[10] 1 Timothy i. 5.
[11] Psalm li. 5.
[12] St. John xix. 26–7.
[13] Hebrews i. 12.
[14] St. Luke vi. 31.
[15] Ibid. x. 38–42.
[16] Ibid. i. 28.
[17] Ibid. i. 42.
[18] Ibid. i. 41.
[19] Ibid. ii. 7.
[20] Isaiah ix. 6.
[21] St. Luke ii. 14.
[22] St. Matthew ii. 1.
[23] The meeting with the good thief is told in the apocryphal 'Arabic Gospel of the Infancy' and in the 'Gospel of Nicodemus or Acts of Pilate'. The good thief is called Titus or Dysmas, and the bad one Dumachus or Gestas. Saint Aelred was probably familiar with the 'Gospel of Nicodemus' which was early in circulation in a Latin translation. Cf. *The Apocryphal New Testament*, ed. Montague Rhodes James, Oxford, 1926, pp. 81 *et seq.*
[24] St. Luke xxiii. 40.
[25] Ibid. xxiii. 42.
[26] Ibid. ii. 48.
[27] Ibid. iv. 2.
[28] St. John viii. 7.
[29] St. Luke vii. 36.
[30] Psalm xiii. 1; Psalm li. 12; Psalm xxvii. 8.
[31] St. Mark ii. 5.
[32] St Matthew xx. 15.
[33] St. John xi. 5.
[34] Ibid. xii. 3.
[35] St. Mark xiv. 5.

NOTES

[36] St. John xii. 13.
[37] Ibid. xiii. 5.
[38] Ibid. xiii. 23.
[39] Ibid. xvii. 11.
[40] St. Matthew xxvi. 38.
[41] St. John xviii. 10.
[42] St. Luke xxii. 62.
[43] Isaiah liii. 7.
[44] St. John xix. 5.
[45] Isaiah ix. 6.
[46] Psalm xliv. 7 (Vulgate).
[47] St. Matthew xxvii. 51.
[48] St. Luke xxiii. 34.
[49] St. Matthew xxvii. 55
[50] St. John xix. 34.
[51] Canticle iv. 3.
[52] Canticle i. 13.
[53] St. John xx. 1.
[54] Ibid. xx. 16.
[55] Ibid. xx. 17.
[56] St. Matthew xxviii. 9.
[57] Genesis iv. 14.
[58] Ibid. xxxvii. 33.
[59] Ecclesiasticus vii. 14 (Vulgate).
[60] St. Matthew vi. 29.
[61] Revelation xiv. 13.
[62] Isaiah xiv. 18.
[63] Psalm cxvi. 15.
[64] Isaiah xiv. 19 (Vulgate).
[65] Proverbs xxxi. 21 (Vulgate)
[66] Psalm lv. 5.
[67] St. Matthew xxv. 34.
[68] St. John xiv. 21.
[69] Ibid. xvii. 3.
[70] 1 Corinthians ii. 9.
[71] Canticle ii. 16.